CHARLES I & CROMWELL TIME LINE

~1599~
Oliver Cromwell born

~1600~
Charles I born

~1603~
James VI of Scotland becomes first Stuart king of England as James I

~1604~
James commissions new English translation of Bible

~1605~
Gunpowder Plot; a Catholic attempt to blow up Parliament

CHARLES' CORONATION

Charles' coronation took place at Westminster Abbey on 2 February 1626. He had married Henrietta Maria the previous year, shortly after acceding to the throne, but it was not, initially, a love match. They seemed incompatible in almost every way. Charles was relatively handsome, while Henrietta was quite plain; she was a devout Catholic while he was a Protestant. Henrietta was so devout that she refused to attend Charles's Protestant coronation service.

FASTIDIOUS APPEARANCE

Charles was a very fastidious person, always conscious of his appearance. Unlike his father (who is supposed never to have washed), Charles paid considerable attention to his personal hygiene. He liked to have his hair, wigs and beard carefully trimmed and styled by a barber, using similar equipment to that shown here on the right.

FAMILY MAN

Whenever possible, Charles liked to spend time with his wife and children, and liked nothing better than to play games with them in the royal nursery. When he was imprisoned during the Civil War (*see pages 18-19*), Charles felt it was important that his children were aware of the full circumstances leading up to his trial (and eventual execution). He insisted that they visit him whenever possible throughout his imprisonment.

CHARLES I
EARLY LIFE

Charles came to the throne at 25 years of age. A shy man of diminutive stature (some accounts state he was just under 1.5 metres tall), he was also very intelligent and a great patron of the arts. He displayed a dignified air and good manners, far removed from the appalling personal habits of his father, James I. Charles was a reserved and very private man and the populace never really took him to their hearts. This, coupled with the Stuart family belief in the "Divine Right of Kings" (*see page 5*), ensured that later on in his reign he became very unpopular. In Scotland the monarchy still retained more of its absolute power, but in England this had been gradually whittled away.

CHANGING DESTINY

Charles was born on 19 November 1600 at Dunfermline Palace, Fife. He was a sickly child who inherited his father's lack of confidence, stammering when nervous. As the second son of James I and Anne of Denmark, Charles was not born to be king. His eldest brother, Henry, was a popular figure who did not seem to carry the family traits of arrogance and physical ungainliness. Unfortunately, Henry died of typhoid in 1612. Had he lived, the course of British history might have been altogether different.

THE YOUNG KING

Charles did not want to become king, but he accepted his responsibilities with honour and dignity. He was always very much aware of his duties as monarch. Unfortunately, his shyness was often perceived as haughty arrogance, which did not endear him to the people. At court, he insisted on preserving his stateliness by not allowing anyone, except his queen, to sit in his presence. This infuriated those who did not like him, particularly Parliamentarians.

SCOTTISH DESCENT

ANNE OF DENMARK

On 23 November 1589, James VI married Anne of Denmark in Oslo. Together they had nine children. It was a marriage of convenience that did not endear the king to his new English subjects.

*C*harles was a Stuart – one of the most powerful royal families ever to rule Scotland. The first Stuart monarch was Robert II, formerly the High Steward of Scotland and the Scottish hero Robert Bruce's grandson. The Stuarts were an ambitious family who were also great patrons of the arts. They elevated Scotland to the forefront of artistic and cultural development in Europe. They were also the last royal dynasty to rule an independent Scotland and were distant relatives of the Tudors. James VI of Scotland (Charles's father) was the great-grandson of Henry VIII's sister Margaret Tudor and James IV of Scotland. When Elizabeth I of England died in 1603, her closest living relative was James VI, King of Scotland, who was invited to take the English throne. He became James I of England, and so united the crowns of the two countries.

MARY QUEEN OF SCOTS (1542-67)

Mary was just one week old when she succeeded to the Scottish throne in 1542. In 1548 she was sent to France where she was brought up by her mother's family. In 1558 Mary married the French Dauphin and became, briefly, Queen of France when he became King Francis II. Francis died in 1560 and Mary returned to Scotland the following year. She later married her cousin Henry, Lord Darnley, and became implicated in a plot to seize the throne of England from Elizabeth I, another of her cousins. She was arrested for treason and imprisoned by Elizabeth for 19 years, before being executed in 1587 in the Tower of London.

"DIVINE RIGHT OF KINGS"

Charles inherited his father's belief in the "Divine Right of Kings"; a doctrine upheld by the entire Stuart dynasty. They believed in the theory that kings were chosen by God to rule and that only God could overrule them. Charles also believed that he alone had the right to make and unmake laws, and to oppose his will was a sin against God.

ROYAL PALACE

Stirling Castle stands at the gateway to the Highlands and was always considered the most vital possession during Scotland's wars of independence. It was built around the 11th century, but the earliest part of the castle to survive dates from the 15th century, when the Stuarts converted the medieval fortress into a magnificent royal palace.

STUART FAMILY TREE

Robert II (1371-90)

Robert III (1390-1406)

James I (1406-37)

James II (1437-60)

James III (1460-88)

James IV (1488-1513)

James V (1513-42)

Mary Queen of Scots (1542-67)

James VI (1567-1625)
(became James I of England - 1603-25)

Charles I (1625-1649)

JAMES VI OF SCOTLAND (JAMES I OF ENGLAND)

James VI succeeded to the Scottish throne in 1567 when his mother, Mary Queen of Scots, was arrested. James was just one year old so until he reached the age of 14, the country was ruled on his behalf by a figure called a regent. In 1603 he succeeded to the English throne on the death of the last Tudor monarch, Elizabeth.

STONE OF SCONE

For centuries, the kings of Scotland had been crowned at Scone Abbey. The ceremonial coronation stone (a large, rectangular boulder believed to date from prehistoric times), formerly kept at the Abbey, was seized by Edward I of England in 1296 when he declared himself king of Scotland. It was taken to Westminster, where it was placed beneath the coronation throne (shown here). It remained in London for 700 years before being returned to Edinburgh in 1996.

LIFE IN STUART BRITAIN

WATER SUPPLIES

Fresh drinking water was difficult to obtain. In towns, most people bought their supplies from water-carriers who transported water in from the country. Communal wells were also common in towns, but the supplies were often contaminated, causing diseases such as typhoid and cholera.

The Stuart age was a period of great change. Improved agricultural methods meant that fewer people were needed to work the land. Many peasants were evicted from their farms, the majority of whom moved to the towns in search of work. This resulted in serious overcrowding in the towns, which in turn led to outbreaks of disease. Fire was one of the biggest risks as most buildings were made of wood and thatch. Streets were narrow, which allowed flames to spread quickly. This happened in the Great Fire of London, which changed the architectural landscape of this great city forever.

LIFE FOR THE RICH

A growing number of people became very wealthy indeed during the reign of the Stuarts. This was mostly as a result of increased foreign trade and exploitation as Britain's empire began to grow. Many nobles replaced their austere castles with magnificent mansions, preferring light, airy rooms. They spared no expense on their new homes, filling them with fine furnishings.

UNHEALTHY LIFESTYLE

Periodic outbreaks of the Bubonic Plague had been a problem since the 14th century, but the plague that occurred in the 1660s was one of the worst on record. Over 100,000 Londoners died in the 1665 outbreak alone. Diseases such as the plague were seen by many (especially the Puritans) as divine punishment from God. Child mortality was high; over half of those born died within their first year. Only one person in 10 could expect to reach the age of 40.

PASTIMES

Although life was hard in Stuart times and annual summer holidays were unheard of, there were a number of official "holy-days", when no-one was expected to work. People played games for fun, rather than competitive sports. The theatre was popular with people of all classes. The rich preferred masques (a combination of music, drama and dance) while the poor opted for bawdy plays.

KING JAMES BIBLE

In 1604, Charles's father, James I, set 54 scholars to work on a new translation of the Holy Bible. It was published in 1611, using a vocabulary of just 5,000 words (one-third of that used by Shakespeare) to make it readable by all classes. The work of Anglican and Puritan ministers, James hoped the new Bible would unite the nation, but most Catholics disliked it, and the book caused further religious division.

CHARLES & GOVERNMENT

*C*harles always had a somewhat fractious relationship with Parliament. At the root of the problem was his belief in the "Divine Right of Kings" (*see page 5*) and his assertion that he should be allowed to rule without question or hindrance from anyone; least of all Parliament. He genuinely believed that a dictatorship was the only effective form of government, and that he was the only one with the nation's interests at heart. Even a bad king, he argued, was better than a rabble of Parliamentarians who had not been schooled to care for a country in the same way as royalty. Moreover, he argued that a king exerted a controlling influence over individual excesses and was less susceptible to corruption. Whatever the rights and wrongs of his view, he was distinctly out of step with political thinking at the time. This put him on a collision course with Parliament.

RELATIONS WITH PARLIAMENT

Charles' character was a strange mixture that did not immediately endear him to others. In private he was polite, intelligent and kindly, yet in public he was often brusque, obstinate and impetuous. This put him at a great disadvantage when dealing with officials, where a certain degree of tact and diplomacy was called for.

CHARLES ABOLISHES PARLIAMENT

Shortly after the death of the Duke of Buckingham, Charles decided to dismiss Parliament. He had been on a collision course with Parliament for some time and was furious when, in 1628, he had been forced to acknowledge the Petition of Right (*see page 11*). When the agreement began to break down the following year, Charles dissolved Parliament altogether. He stubbornly refused to summon the House again and ruled on his own for 11 years.

THE LONG & THE SHORT OF IT

Charles' rule without Parliament became increasingly difficult as time went on. He had become virtually bankrupt and did not have control of his own army, so when rebellion broke out in Scotland Charles was unable to contain it and was forced to ask for assistance. Reluctantly, the king recalled Parliament in 1640, but peace was short-lived. Charles dismissed the new parliament after just three weeks, and it became known afterwards as the "Short Parliament". The situation worsened, however, and Charles was forced to recall Parliament again. This attempt was more successful and the house remained in office until 1653. It became known as the "Long Parliament" and was finally dismissed by Oliver Cromwell for being incompetent.

THE KING RULES ALONE

Charles ruled alone, without Parliament, for a period of 11 years, between 1629-40. In order to overcome any political or religious opposition to his "divine" rule, he gave additional power to the Court of Star Chamber (shown left) and the Court of High Commission (shown right), to support his actions. Both of these institutions served as a royal council and were made up of officials, justices and advisors. Their job was to administer any new laws passed, to hear petitions and deal with complaints. When Parliament was recalled into office it was felt that the king had abused the power of these courts, so in 1641 both the Court of Star Chamber and Court of High Commission were abolished to prevent further corruption.

PETITION OF RIGHT

In February 1628, Parliament forced Charles to acknowledge the Petition of Right, giving Parliament certain liberties, whilst taking away the absolutism of royal power. Its four main demands were that taxation should be levied only with parliamentary consent; no-one should be jailed without trial; martial law should be abolished; and no troops should be billeted in private households. Charles was furious at having to make this concession and it became the main bone of contention between King and Parliament.

*N*o single event can be cited as the direct cause of the Civil War. Instead, it was a gradual build up of mistrust between King and Parliament that finally came to a head when all other avenues of compromise had failed. With the growing strength of a democratic parliament in England and the medieval attitude of "divine right" still pursued by Charles I, it was perhaps inevitable that the growing disagreement would ultimately lead to armed conflict. Charles hated the whole notion of parliaments, feeling that a dictatorial monarch, however bad, was preferable to the indecision of government by committee. Despite his shyness and retiring nature, Charles was often hot-headed and hasty. It was his ill-conceived attempt to arrest five members of Parliament that became the spark which ignited this tinderbox of discontent.

SHIP MONEY

Ship Money was a tax levied by the crown on coastal towns to help keep the Royal Navy afloat. This cause an uproar, however, and in 1636 the Parliamentarian John Hampden refused to pay the tax. At a specially convened court the following year he was ordered to pay, but it was also acknowledged that the king had acte illegally, outside the provisions of the Petition of Right, an his authority was called into question.

THE EARL OF STRAFFORD

Thomas Wentworth, Earl of Strafford, was a turncoat who paid for his treachery with his life. He was instrumental in forcing Charles to agree to the Petition of Right, but then he switched loyalty to the king. Between 1633-40 he was Charles' deputy in Ireland, where he enforced a brutal regime against the Irish and soon became one of the most hated men in the country. Parliament forced the king to sign a Bill of Attainder condemning the Earl to death. Thomas Wentworth was executed on 12 May 1641.

ENGLISH PRAYER BOOK

William Laud was made Archbishop in 1633 to help endorse King Charles's religious policies. He quickly aroused the hatred of the Puritans with his views. In 1637 he decided to impose the English Prayer Book on Scotland. The Scots were mostly Presbyterian (a version of Christianity similar to the Puritans) and they hated bishops and prayer books, which they saw as "popery". These actions were a primary cause of the Civil War.

SCOTTISH RIOTS

As a direct result of Laud's plan to impose the English Prayer Book on Scotland, the Scots erupted into open rebellion. The king was unable to raise a sufficiently strong force to put down the riots. Reluctantly, in 1640, the virtually bankrupt Charles was forced to recall Parliament and ask for their help. It was an event that was to lead to the final confrontation between King and Parliament.

CHARLES ARRESTS MPS

The actual event that started the Civil War occurred in January 1642 when Charles marched into the House of Commons and tried to arrest five leading MPs who seemed to oppose the king's every move. The MPs had been forewarned, however, and had already fled. Fearing he had himself gone too far, Charles fled to the North for his own safety. In his absence, the country began to divide itself between King and Parliament, and by August that same year Charles felt strong enough to raise his standard at Nottingham in defiance of Parliament. The Civil War had begun.

CHARLES I & CROMWELL TIME LINE

~1611~
Authorized version of the Bible published

~1612~
Henry, Prince of Wales, dies

Charles becomes heir to throne

~1625~
James I dies

Charles succeeds to the throne

~1626~
Charles dissolves Parliament

~1628~
Duke of Buckingham is assassinated

Petition of Right issued, limiting royal power

Cromwell enters politics for first time

~1629~
Charles dissolves Parliament again

THE NATION DIVIDED

Most of the prosperous south-east, including London, supported Parliament. The king, on the other hand, had established a base at Oxford, and had support in much of Wales, and the north and west of England. Initially, Scotland too supported the king, but they switched their allegiance later on in the war.

CHARLES I & CROMWELL TIME LINE

~1637~

Charles tries to force new English Prayer Book on Scots

~1640~

Charles summons the Short Parliament, which lasts three weeks

Scots cross the border and defeat the king's army at Newburn

Charles summons the Long Parliament

~1641~

Star Chamber and Court of High Commission abolished

~1642~

Charles tries unsuccessfully to arrest five MPs

Outbreak of Civil War

Royalists win Battle of Powick Bridge

The Battle of Edgehill

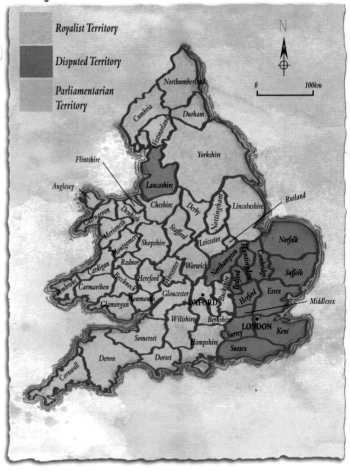

Royalist Territory

Disputed Territory

Parliamentarian Territory

N

0   100km

Northumberland

Cumbria

Westmorland

Durham

Yorkshire

Flintshire

Anglesey

Lancashire

Caernarvon

Denbigh

Cheshire

Derby

Nottingham

Lincolnshire

Rutland

Merioneth

Stafford

Montgomery

Shropshire

Leicester

Norfolk

Cardigan

Radnor

Worcester

Warwick

Northampton

Huntingdon

Cambridge

Suffolk

Pembroke

Carmarthen

Brecknock

Hereford

Buckingham

Bedford

Essex

Glamorgan

Monmouth

Gloucester

OXFORD

Hertford

Middlesex

Wiltshire

Berkshire

LONDON

Kent

Somerset

Hampshire

Surrey

Sussex

Devon

Dorset

Cornwall

BATTLE OF EDGEHILL

The Battle of Edgehill was the first major engagement of the Civil War. It was the first time since the Wars of the Roses, nearly 200 years earlier, that fellow countrymen had fought one another on English soil. The battle began when the royalist and parliamentarian armies faced each other in Warwickshire on 23 October 1642. Both armies suffered losses but the setting sun and exhaustion on both sides made futher fighting impossible. On the following day, the Parliamentarians withdrew, with neither side able to claim victory.

RAISING THE ROYAL STANDARD

In 1642, both the king and parliament set about to gain control over castles, opposition's forces and their weapons. Both sides had now built up small armies and so skirmishes broke out, but it wasn't until the king raised his standard at Nottingham Castle in the August that the war had officially began.

THE CIVIL WAR
1642: THE OUTBREAK

When the Civil War broke out in 1642, there was no nationally organized army. Both the Royalist and Parliamentarian armies were comprised of ordinary men – mostly farmers or labourers – with little or no military experience. They were also expected to provide their own weapons, which meant that both sides were initially very poorly equipped. The nation divided itself between supporters of the Royalist and Parliamentarian causes. Often families were divided in their loyalties, with brother fighting against brother and father against son. There was also a deeper social divide – that of religion. Catholics tended to support the king, while Protestants, particularly Puritans, mostly supported Parliament.

PRINCE RUPERT

In the early period of the Civil War, the Royalists were much better equipped and trained than the Parliamentarians. They quickly gained the upper hand, thanks to the military skills of such loyal supporters as Prince Rupert, the German-born nephew of Charles I. Rupert came to his uncle's aid at the age of just 23. He had gained experience of wars in Europe and so Charles made him commander of the royalist cavalry. He specialized in lightning cavalry charges, in which his lightly-armed soldiers attacked the Parliamentarians at full gallop, making maximum use of the element of surprise. Rupert's forces won a minor battle at Powick Bridge in September 1642, which established his reputation as an outstanding military commander.

THE CIVIL WAR
ON THE BATTLEFIELD

*I*n popular imagination the Civil War was fought between "Cavaliers" and "Roundheads". In reality, however, these terms only came into common usage towards the end of the conflict and even then they were used as insults. The king's supporters were usually courtiers, noble gentleman who attended the royal court and were chivalrous and flamboyantly dressed. Many Parliamentary supporters were Puritans, who opted for simpler and plainer clothes. But there were many nobles who supported Parliament and Puritans who supported the king. On the battlefield, there was little to tell the two sides apart. Officers on both sides were often wealthy and wore fine clothes, while ordinary soldiers were generally poor and had no uniforms. To overcome this problem, coloured sashes or armbands were worn so soldiers could tell friend from foe.

CAVALIERS & ROUNDHEADS

The King's supporters were called Cavaliers because of their flamboyant clothing of lace collars, feathered hats, knee-length boots and fine doublets. The Parliamentarians were called Roundheads because of the uniform of the New Model Army (*see page 19*), which consisted of red tunics, metal breastplates and round, metal helmets.

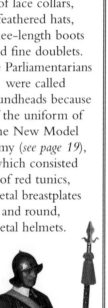

SWITCHING SIDES

Many of the soldiers enlisted by both sides were untrained and apolitical. They joined up because of promises of uniforms and pay. However, it was common for these promises to be broken and soldiers often changed sides, even on the battlefield. Other soldiers defected if they were on the losing side in a battle. They would surrender and agree to fight for the victors. It was a hard life for soldiers on both sides. They had to march long distances, sleep rough and kill their own food. Surprisingly low numbers actually died on the battlefield – most died at the hands of "surgeons", who knew little about germs or infection.

BRING YOUR PIKE & MUSKET

Pikemen were foot soldiers and their main role was to protect the musketeers. During a cavalry charge, pikemen would form a circle around the musketeers with their long pikes pointing out. The cavalry horses refused to charge into such danger and they often unseated their riders. If this happened, the musketeers would then use their muskets as clubs to kill the fallen cavalrymen.

A FRIGHTENING SIGHT

Both armies comprised three main elements: pikemen, musketeers and cavalry. Armed with swords and pistols and mounted on horseback, the cavalry regiments were the cream of the fighting force. They were often nobility or gentlemen, experienced hunters who could afford horses. At a charge, the cavalry were a terrifying sight!

GUNPOWDER, BULLET & SHOT

Muskets were very slow-loading guns and they were not very accurate. Gunpowder was poured down the barrel of the musket with a lead bullet or "shot". A small amount of gunpowder was put into a pan at the trigger end and then ignited, firing the gun. It usually took an experienced musketeer 20 minutes to reload his weapon. Cannons were much more deadly. Large cannons were used during sieges, while smaller cannons were used on the battlefield.

THE CIVIL WAR
1643-4: WAR PROGRESSES

EARL OF ESSEX

If Prince Rupert was the key military figure in the Royalist army, the Parliamentarians had Robert Devereux, the Earl of Essex. Like Prince Rupert, he had gained military experience in Europe as a high-ranking commander. His reputation was established when he defeated the king's army at Newbury in September 1643. The king withdrew because his supplies were low and Essex returned to London a hero.

The Civil War was actually three wars. The first conflict was the most serious, and took place between 1642–6. What began as an uprising in Scotland soon escalated into a war that involved all four nations. Up until the winter of 1643, the war seemed to be going the Royalist's way, but in 1944 Parliament signed an agreement with the Scots Parliament, and suddenly the king had a new and formidable threat from the north.

THE QUEEN'S MOVE

Before leaving London for Royalist territory in the north, Charles had made sure that Queen Henrietta was safely on a boat for Holland. She had taken many of the crown jewels with her, which she sold to buy arms to help her husband. A year later, Henrietta returned with ammunition and money. She went to York and began assembling a small army, which she then took to Charles in Oxford.

OXFORD: THE ROYALIST CAPITAL

In August 1642, the King was based in Nottingham. However, he was anxious to open up the important route to London. As he moved south, Essex's army went after him, so Charles stopped in Oxford to set up a base and garrison. By then Essex had overtaken the king and lay in wait with 20,000 men at Turnham Green. Charles was forced to retreat to Oxford, which then became the Royalist capital.

Main battle sites
1642-1646

MAJOR BATTLE SITES 1642-6

CHARLES I &
CROMWELL TIME LINE

~1643~

Siege of Gloucester

First Battle of Newbury

Scots and Parliament
become allies

~1644~

Cromwell appointed
Lieutenant General for
all Parliamentary armies

Scottish army
invades England

Royalist army
defeated at the Battle
of Marston Moor

Battles broke out throughout the country as both sides attempted to swell their armies and raise funding for the war, as well as seize castles, cities and county armouries.

CITY SIEGES

It was a common occurrence during the Civil War for cities to become besieged by opposing forces. They would surround cities and stop food coming in, and its citizens leaving, which led to great hardship. To boost morale, reassure mercenary soldiers and allow everyday life continue, money like these four coins would be produced within besieged cities.

BATTLE OF MARSTON MOOR

The Royalist cavalry, under the command of Prince Rupert remained undefeated until 1644, at the Battle of Marston Moor. Under the control of a young cavalry commander called Oliver Cromwell – and aided by their Scottish allies – the Parliamentarian army won a resounding victory against the Royalists. It was there that Cromwell earned Prince Rupert's respect and he first coined the phrase "ironsides" when describing the Parliamentarian troops. The battle was hugely significant. It gave Parliament a foothold in the North and the Royalists were never to recover from this defeat.

THE CIVIL WAR
THE KING'S CAPTURE

The turning point of the war came in the winter of 1944, after the second Battle of Newbury. The combined armies of Parliament's main commanders – the Earl of Essex, Sir William Waller and the Earl of Manchester – failed to defeat the outnumbered Royalist army. To make matters worse, disagreement between Manchester and his second in command, Oliver Cromwell, spilled over into Parliament, creating two factions – those who wanted to defeat the King and those who wanted peace. There was also a religious division between those who wanted Presbyterianism to be the one religion and those (including Cromwell) who preferred the idea of religious independence for all. Eventually a combined, national force called the New Model Army was created to unite all sides. It was commanded by Sir Thomas Fairfax, with Oliver Cromwell as his second-in-command.

SIR THOMAS FAIRFAX

One of the leading military commanders for Parliament was Sir Thomas Fairfax. He was appointed Lieutenant-General of the New Model Army in 1645 and, together with Oliver Cromwell, was largely responsible for Parliament's eventual victory. During the Civil War, Leeds Castle in Kent (left), was used as an arsenal for Parliament and so escaped the usual "slighting" (dismantling) after the war. This magnificent castle later passed into the hands of the Fairfax family by marriage.

THE NEW MODEL ARMY

The New Model Army changed the course of the Civil War. The army was organized on a national basis and received regular wages, the first fighting force to do so. Soldiers were well-equipped and well-trained. Officers were promoted to rank based on their abilities, rather than on their social standing.

BATTLE OF NASEBY

The Battle of Naseby marked the real turning point in the conflict and effectively ended the war. It took place in June 1645 and though the war dragged on until 1649, the Royalists were a spent force after the conflict at Naseby. The battle saw the first engagement of Parliament's New Model Army. At 15,000 strong and twice the size of the Royalist army, Parliament completely overwhelmed their rivals.

CHARLES I'S IMPRISONMENT

Following Charles's defeat at Naseby, the king fled to Scotland, but the Scots betrayed him and handed him over to Parliament. He managed to escape but was soon recaptured and, in November 1647, was imprisoned in Carisbrooke Castle on the Isle of Wight (left). Charles enjoyed relative freedom there, receiving frequent visitors, including his close family (right). The king negotiated with Parliament to secure his release and, at the same time, he secretly organized an invasion of England by the Scottish army. This sparked off the second Civil War. However, royalist forces were defeated by Cromwell at Preston in August 1648, leaving the king at the mercy of Parliament.

THE KING'S EXECUTION

THE KING ON TRIAL

The trial of Charles I was held at Westminster Hall. It began on 20 January 1649, and lasted just one week. Charles reportedly said to friends that if he had been unable to live as a king, he might at least die a gentleman. He refused to acknowledge the legality of the court and refused to plead, stating: *"I do stand more for the liberty of my people than any that come here to be my pretended judges."*

*W*hile Charles I was imprisoned in Carisbrooke Castle, his supporters valiantly continued to fight for his cause. However, Charles had made several serious tactical errors throughout the conflict (one of the bloodiest in British history) that meant the war was already lost. Cromwell's forces won the day, and the king paid with his life. He was tried and executed for treason within a week in January 1649.

DEATH WARRANT

Above is the death warrant of Charles I. It was signed by 59 specially chosen republicans, and stated that the king should be executed by beheading. Many Republicans shrank from signing the warrant, feeling that imprisonment was punishment enough. The news of Charles' impending execution sent shock waves throughout Europe.

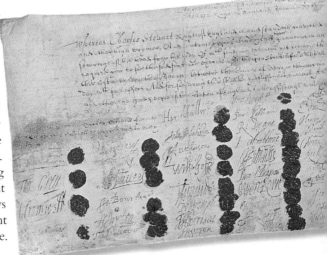

SAD FAREWELLS

Throughout his trial Charles had been confined to a house near to Westminster Palace, where he was allowed to spend time with his wife and children. His two eldest sons were safely exiled in France, but Henry, Duke of Gloucester, and Princess Elizabeth, were locked up with their father. Before he died, Charles gave Elizabeth a message for Henrietta Maria, to be passed on after his death. It stated that he had always thought of her and loved her to the end.

DIGNIFIED TO THE END

Even after the Royalist cause had been lost, Charles stubbornly refused to accept defeat, to repent of his actions or to acknowledge republican authority. He also refused to change his views on the monarchy and the Church, forcing some of Cromwell's more fanatical supporters to call for his execution. Charles rose magnificently to the occasion. Dressed entirely in black he remained dignified throughout the proceedings. His last words were: *"I needed not to have come here…I am the martyr of the people."*

EXECUTION

Sentence was passed on Charles on 27 January 1649. He was given just three days to put his affairs in order before his execution on 30 January. The king's friend, Bishop Juxon, administered his last Holy Communion. Charles spent his last night with his family at St. James's Palace, and at 10am the next morning he was escorted to Whitehall. The execution took place at 2pm. When the axe fell, a groan went around the crowd and his severed head was held aloft for all to see.

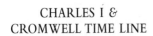
~1649~

Charles is tried and
executed by beheading

Council of State
appointed with Oliver
Cromwell as Chairman

England declared
a Republic

Irish Royalists
defeated by Cromwell

~1650~

Scots Royalists
defeated by Cromwell

~1651~

Scots Royalists
led by Charles II
(who claims the
throne) defeated
at Worcester

Charles II
flees to
France
in exile

Navigation
Act gives
monopoly
to English
ships

A RELIGOUS MAN

Cromwell was a deeply religious
man, who believed that his
actions were guided by God.
This belief made him extremely
indecisive at times, but it also made
Cromwell determined to carry
through his beliefs, whatever
the consequences. For a
while, Cromwell choose
to overlook religious
and political dissent,
but his patience
deteriorated as
he got older.

MILITARY GENIUS

Cromwell was a self-taught soldier
who learned his tactical skills by
reading military accounts of great
battles. At the outset of the Civil
War he led a cavalry unit in East
Anglia and quickly rose through
the ranks. By 1644, he was
appointed Lieutenant-
General and the following
year he helped form the New
Model Army. Cromwell was
regarded throughout Europe as
one of the leading commanders
of his day.

OLIVER CROMWELL

EARLY LIFE

Despite his anti-monarchist view, Oliver Cromwell's family were, in fact, of noble ancestry, though Oliver himself never inherited a title. His great-grandfather, Richard Cromwell, acquired vast properties in East Anglia and considerable wealth during the reign of Henry VIII, largely as a result of plundering monasteries. Oliver's grandfather, Sir Henry Cromwell, was known as the "Golden Knight", probably because of his immense wealth. Robert Cromwell, Oliver's father, inherited a small estate in Huntingdon, while his wife Elizabeth was also descended from a noble family. Her father was Sir William Steward, who even claimed a tenuous link to the Stuart royal family.

THE SITE OF CROMWELL'S BIRTH

Oliver Cromwell was born on 25 April 1599 and baptized four days later at the church of St. John the Baptist at Huntingdon. Very little is known about his early life. He was not a particularly academic child, though he did attend Cambridge University for about a year. However, he was forced to leave, without a degree, following the unexpected death of his father. Oliver was just 18 years old when he inherited the family property and took on the responsibility of looking after his mother and unmarried sisters.

COUNCIL OF STATE

Following the execution of King Charles I, the remaining members of the Long Parliament decided to form a Council of State later in 1649. Oliver Cromwell was elected Chairman, but the Council proved a disappointment to him. He soon realized that many of its members were no more interested in parliamentary reform than the king himself had been, and simply meant to further their own needs. They obstructed many of Cromwell's reforms, which prompted him to take matters into his own hands.

THE COMMONWEALTH

*F*ollowing the execution of King Charles I, Britain became (briefly) a republic, but the new system of government was far from satisfactory. In many respects, it bore close similarities to the corrupt monarchical system it aimed to replace. The dominant figure throughout was Oliver Cromwell. This period, known as the Commonwealth, can be divided into two distinct phases. The first, known as the "Republic", spanned the period 1649-53 and was dominated by Cromwell's attempts to govern within the existing parliamentary framework. The second phase was known as the "Protectorate", when Cromwell ruled as virtual dictator.

CROMWELL DISSOLVES PARLIAMENT

In 1653 Cromwell dismissed the Long Parliament because it had become corrupt and kept blocking his reforms. He declared himself Lord Protector and ruled with his New Model Army, a Council of 15 and a Protectorate Parliament of 400. In all, three Parliaments were set up by Cromwell, but each was dismissed as it failed to live up to his ideals and blocked his plans for reform.

CROMWELL OFFERED THE THRONE

In 1657 Cromwell was offered the crown of England by the Protectorate Parliament. By inviting him to become king, Parliament hoped to unite a country still deeply divided behind a common cause. Cromwell refused, saying that he was against the principle of hereditary rule. More importantly, perhaps, his own generals were also against the idea and threatened to revolt if he accepted. Cromwell was offered the crown several more times, but each time he refused.

BATTLE OF DUNBAR

The Civil War did not end completely with the execution of Charles I. Hostilities dragged on for another two years. The Scots, dissatisfied at their treatment by Parliament, switched their allegiance once again and offered their support to the king's son, Charles II. Cromwell defeated them at the Battle of Dunbar in 1650, but the Scots continued to support the Jacobite (Stuart) cause until the Battle of Culloden in 1746.

PURITAN VALUES

Cromwell's Parliament introduced many laws to curb people's waywardness. Churches were stripped of all decoration and their interiors painted white to remove all idolatry. It became compulsory to attend church on Sundays, or face the stocks as punishment. Christmas and Easter celebrations were abolished, along with most forms of entertainment. Some Puritans became almost fanatical in their zeal for religious and political reform. One of these was Matthew Hopkins (left), the self-appointed "Witchfinder General", who conducted a series of trials between 1644-6 in which over 200 supposed witches were put to death.

OLIVER CROMWELL

THE LATER YEARS

As he grew older, Cromwell became more and more disillusioned with life. He became increasingly uncertain that his actions had been right. Parliament had proved itself to be as corrupt and as obstructive as the monarchy, and Cromwell had been unable to carry through the political reforms he had wanted. Furthermore, he knew that he had been ruling as a virtual dictator, king in all but name, and that his dreams of a true democracy lay shattered. Britain's first brush with radical social reform had come to nothing. Although Cromwell himself was more liberal than many might suppose, the puritans who carried out many social reforms in his name were becoming hated by the people, who saw their reforms as stifling.

PURITANICAL GOVERNMENT

After he became Lord Protector, Cromwell called his first Parliament, which sat in 1654. The following year he dismissed it and ruled instead with the army. He divided the country into 11 districts, each one ruled by a Major-General.

CARICATURE

Oliver Cromwell was neither a handsome nor a popular figure, even though he was generally acknowledged as a military genius and the man thought most capable of leading a nation that had been so bitterly divided. King Charles's trial and execution had been, to a large degree, unexpected. Most had expected the king simply to be deposed and imprisoned. His execution was certainly not met with the jubilation Parliament had expected. Even Cromwell seems to have been reluctant for things to have gone so far. Often the subject of derision, this caricature of Cromwell depicts him as a country squire, almost as a simpleton.

STATESMAN

Oliver Cromwell did not become a statesman through his military prowess alone, as is often supposed. Having already played an active role in local government, in 1628 he was chosen to be one of the representatives of Huntingdon in Parliament. It was the fourth year of Charles' reign and already the king had called three Parliaments. Cromwell's entry into politics thus coincided with the king's fall from popularity and the beginning of the real difficulties between King and State. In his first session in Parliament, Cromwell added his support to the passing of the Petition of Right, which guaranteed certain Parliamentary liberties and fired Cromwell's passion for political reform.

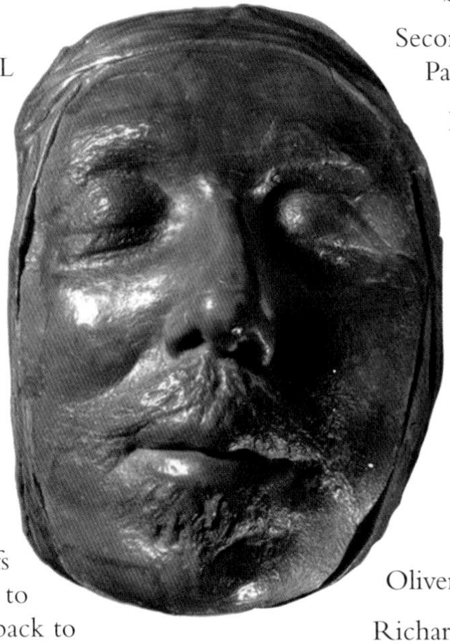

CROMWELL DIES

Oliver Cromwell died on 3rd September 1658. He had suffered attacks of colic, gout and recurring bouts of malaria throughout his life (the latter probably the cause of his death). It was rumoured that his Puritan beliefs would not allow physicians to administer a powder, brought back to Europe by Catholic priests from Spain, which might have treated his ailments. He was buried in state at Westminster Abbey, but his body was horrifically disinterred two years later and hanged at Tyburn by supporters of Charles II following his restoration. The severed head of his corpse was publicly displayed on the roof of Westminster Hall an undignified end to a glittering career. Picture above is Cromwell's death mask.

CHARLES I & CROMWELL TIME LINE

~1652~
First Dutch war breaks out

~1653~
Cromwell expels the Long (Rump) Parliament

Cromwell declares himself Lord Protector of England

~1654~
First Protectorate Parliament called

~1655~
Cromwell dismisses Parliament, rules with army and 11 Major-Generals

~1656~
Second Protectorate Parliament called

Rule by the 11 Major-Generals is abolished

~1657~
Cromwell refuses offer to take throne

~1658~
Cromwell dismisses Third Protectorate Parliament

Oliver Cromwell dies.

Richard Cromwell succeeds

~1659~
Richard Cromwell resigns

~1660~
Charles II returns to take the throne

WARS WITH EUROPE

HUGUENOT REFUGEES

The spread of Protestantism throughout Europe caused much unrest. In France over 60,000 Protestants (known as Huguenots) were forcibly converted to Catholicism in 1682. In 1685 it became illegal for Protestants to freely practice religion. They were openly persecuted and many Huguenot refugees fled France and settled in England.

*O*ne of the most important consequences to come from the Civil War was Britain's rise to power on the international stage. Throughout Europe, British commanders such as Cromwell and Fairfax were widely respected, and the emergence of the New Model Army held most of Britain's adversaries in awe. At sea, brilliant commanders such as Robert Blake won numerous victories. Within two years of Cromwell's death the Commonwealth began to collapse, but Britain prospered under Charles II and continued to exert its influence abroad.

SIEGE OF DROGHEDA

Following Charles I's execution, the Irish and Scots led a combined rebellion against Parliament. For both countries it was seen as the ideal opportunity to free themselves from English rule, once and for all. In response, Cromwell sent a massive force over to Ireland, defeating them at the sieges of Wexford and Drogheda in 1649.

THE DUTCH WARS

In 1651 Parliament passed the Navigation Act. It gave English merchant ships a monopoly over trade from English ports. This bolstered the English economy but caused immediate distress to the Dutch. War broke out with Holland in 1652, but the Dutch navy was defeated by the brilliant English commander, Robert Blake.

WARS WITH FRANCE & SPAIN

Britain also found itself at war with France and Spain at various times after the end of the Civil War. Both countries (still largely Catholic and loyal to the Royalist cause) had leant their support to Charles during the course of the Civil War and Parliament wished to exert its new-found authority over them. Several of

these skirmishes occurred in the colonies, where Britain was looking to build its dominions into an empire. Jamaica was successfully taken from the Spanish in 1655 and several victories were won against France in North America.

BORN TO BE KING

Charles's eldest son, Charles II, was born in 1630. Following his father's execution, Charles continued to fight against Parliament, but eventually lost to Cromwell at the Battle of Worcester in 1651 and fled to France in exile. Although technically still king, Charles had little money and lived frugally for 11 years. In 1660 he was asked by Parliament to return to England as king. Although Charles II had 14 illegitimate children by his various mistresses, his wife did not provide him with an heir, so when he died in 1685 the throne passed to his younger brother, James.

THE MERRY MONARCH

When Charles II was invited to become king, there were certain conditions imposed on him to prevent royal excesses occurring again. He was also required to marry Catherine of Braganza from Portugal. It was a political and loveless marriage. Charles took many mistresses including Nell Gwynne, whom he openly courted and who is believed to have given him two sons. Charles's return was generally welcomed across the country and his flamboyance was a refreshing contrast to the Puritan rule before him.

JAMES II

Charles's second son, James, had converted to Catholicism in the 1660s and Parliament tried to prevent him from succeeding to the throne. He openly declared his intention to restore Catholicism to England. In 1688, when faced with a series of demands by Parliament to prevent this, he chose to abdicate and went into exile in France. The throne passed, jointly, to his daughter Mary and son-in-law William of Orange, the Dutch ruler.

RETURN OF THE MONARCHY

The act of removing what many saw as a tyrannical monarchy proved an easier task than finding a suitable system of government to replace it. Cromwell and his New Model Army had won the Civil War with little assistance from Parliament, and when he later tried to introduce radical reform, he discovered Parliament was just as corrupt as the monarchy had ever been. He became an extremely strict ruler, and turned many people against the idea of a republic. Within two years of Cromwell's death, Parliament became so unstable it was facing the prospect of another civil war. Charles II was invited to come out of exile in Holland and return home as king. The monarchy was restored.

CROMWELL'S SUCCESSOR

When Oliver Cromwell died in 1658, aged 59, he was succeeded as Lord Protector by his son, Richard, despite his supposed aversion to hereditary rule. Known derisorily as "Tumbledown Dick", he lacked his father's qualities of leadership and integrity. He did not want to be leader and accepted the position reluctantly. Richard was forced to resign the following year.

A NEW KING

When Charles II returned to the English throne in 1660, public opinion had turned away from republican ideals. The surviving 41 republicans who had signed his father's death warrant were called to justice. Most of them fled abroad, or voluntarily surrendered to escape execution, but ten refused to beg forgiveness. They were all tried and sentenced to death.

DID YOU KNOW?

That Charles I refused to show fear, even on the scaffold? Throughout the ordeal of his imprisonment and trial, Charles retained a dignified air and refused either to acknowledge his accusers or show fear of death. On the day of his execution, it was a cold January day and so that he would not shiver and give the impression of being afraid, he requested an extra shirt to keep him warm. The shirt can still be seen in the Museum of London today.

That the nursery rhyme "Goosey, Goosey, Gander" refers to Cromwell? This well-known nursery rhyme is a direct reference to Cromwell and his Roundheads.

"Goosey, goosey, gander,
Whither shall I wander,
Upstairs and downstairs
And in my lady's chamber.
There I met an old man
Who would not say his prayers,
So I took him by the left leg
And threw him down the stairs."

Soldiers in Cromwell's New Model Army were noted for their goose-stepping march. After the Civil War they searched the houses of all known Royalist and Catholic sympathizers looking for Royalist fugitives. Any suspect who refused to accept Puritan ways, or Catholic who refused to accept their Protestant religion, was arrested and thrown into jail.

That Oliver Cromwell invented the term "foolscap" paper? Before the demise of Charles I, paper-making in England was licensed by the king. Every sheet of paper produced carried the royal cypher (or monogram) as a watermark, visible when held up to the light. With his customary contempt for all things royal, Cromwell abolished the royal insignia and replaced it with the cap of a jester (a "fools cap"). Before the advent of metric paper sizes, sheets of typing paper (regardless of the watermark) were known as foolscap.

How the Quakers got their name? The Quakers, originally known as the Children of Light (and now known as the Society of Friends) were founded around the mid-17th century by George Fox. They began as a sect of Protestant extremists, with views even more radical than the Puritans. On one occasion in 1650 Fox appeared in court accused of illegal preaching. He defended himself by saying that the judge, not he, would incur God's wrath. To which the judge replied that he was not afraid and that the only "quaker" in court was Fox himself. The term stuck. There is an alternative version that says the name is derived from believers quaking with religious fervour during prayer readings.

That the fate of Charles I was predicted 100 years before? The 16th-century French prophet, Nostradamus, accurately predicted the outcome of the Civil War in several separate predictions, written in verse. They concern Charles I, Cromwell and Archbishop Laud. In one passage he wrote: *"The Parliament of London will put their king to death. He will die because of the shaven heads in council."* He also foretold the Great Fire of London and gave the precise date of 1666. His predictions were all the more uncanny because they were made 100 years before the event.

ACKNOWLEDGEMENTS

We would like to thank: Graham Rich, Hazel Poole and Elizabeth Wiggans for their assistance.

Copyright © 2003 ticktock Entertainment Ltd.

First published in Great Britain by ticktock Media Ltd., Unit 2, Orchard Business Centre, North Farm Road, Tunbridge Wells, Kent, TN2 3XF. All rights reserved. No part of this publication may be reproduced, stored in a retrieval system, or transmitted in any form or by any means electronic, mechanical, photocopying, recording or otherwise, without prior written permission of the copyright owner.

A CIP catalogue record for this book is available from the British Library. ISBN 1 86007 088 4

Picture research by Image Select.

Printed in Egypt.

snapping-turtle guide